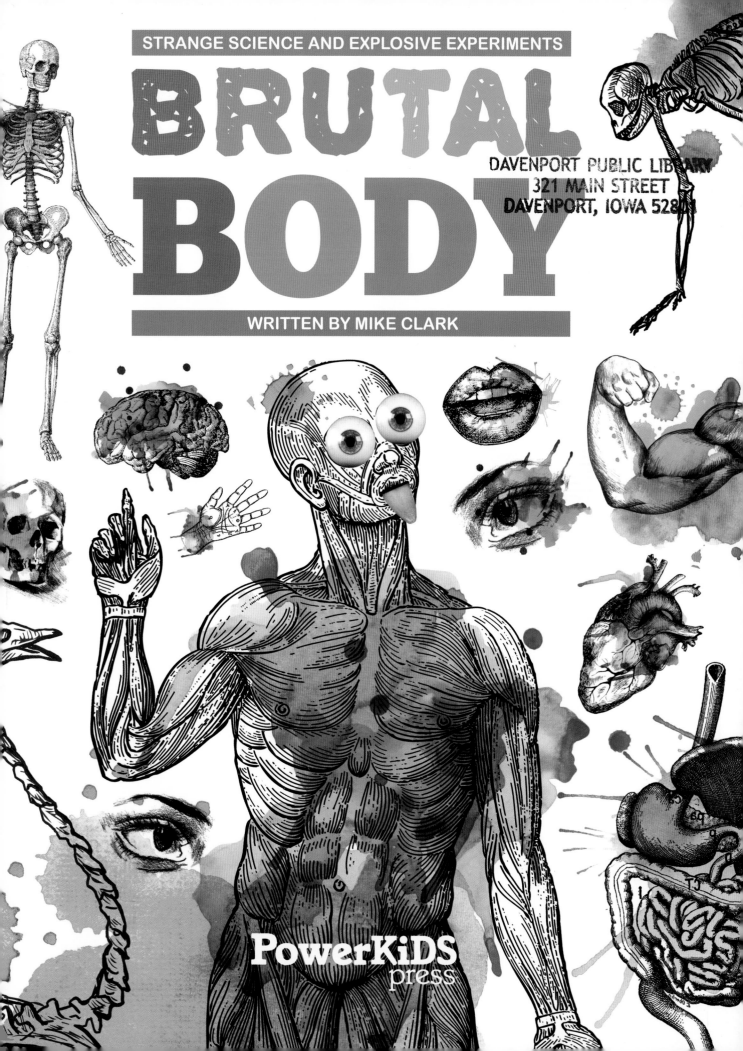

STRANGE SCIENCE AND EXPLOSIVE EXPERIMENTS

BRUTAL
BODY

WRITTEN BY MIKE CLARK

PowerKiDS
press

Published in 2018 by
The Rosen Publishing Group, Inc.
29 East 21st Street, New York, NY 10010

Cataloging-in-Publication Data
Names: Clark, Mike.
Title: Brutal body / Mike Clark.
Description: New York : PowerKids Press, 2018. | Series:
   Strange science and explosive experiments | Includes index.
Identifiers: ISBN 9781538323588 (pbk.) | ISBN 9781538322628
   (library bound) | ISBN 9781538323595 (6 pack)
Subjects: LCSH: Human body--Experiments--Juvenile literature.
Classification: LCC QP37.C53 2018 | DDC 612--dc23

Written by: Mike Clark
Edited by: Charlie Ogden
Designed by: Matt Rumbelow

Photo credits: Abbreviations: l-left, r-right, b-bottom, t-top, c-center, m-middle. 2 –
molekuul_be. 4 – Nicola Renna. 5: bg – S K Chavan; tl – Phonlamai Photo, bl – nexus 7.
br – Andrii Vodolazhskyi. 6: t –Trikona; m – oorka; b – Kateryna Kon. 7: bg – Melianiaka
Kanstantsin, front – Lightspring. 8/9 – Romariolen. 9: KaliAntye. 10: tr – Pavel Kubarkov.
10 circles: 1 – Only background; 2 – optimarc; 3 – Tetiana Babinich; 4 – prasit2512; 5 –
Rost9. 11: leungchopan. 14m: 1 – Pim; 2 – Lena Veťka; 3 – Pim; 4 – artsandra. 5 – Natalia
Hubbert. 14b: l – Antonio Guillem; r – Kateryna Kon. 15 – Victoria 1. 16: t – Ruta Production;
ml – Fotofermer; mc – aleg baranau; mr – graja; b – 309782864. 17: tl – Nathalie Speliers
Ufermann; ml – timquo; r – Katya Shut. 18-19: nexus 7. 18: ml – Thana Thanadechakul;
mr – Moteelec. 19: tl – AMB; tc – molekuul_be; tr – molekuul_be. 19m – Danny Smythe. 20:
l – Anatomy Insider; br – nobeastsofierce. 21 – CLIPAREA I Custom media. 22: bl – Andrii
Vodolazhskyi; 22 tr – Jesada Sabai. 23: bg – Andrii Vodolazhskyi; top – Andrea Danti. 24:
t – onair; b – CLIPAREA I Custom media. 25: bg – hannadarzy; t – most popular; b – Ninell.
26: tr – TonTonic. 26 – DoubleBubble. 28: bg – Georgios Kollidas; tr – TonTonic; br – Dudarev
Mikhail. br eyes – Markus Gann.

Manufactured in China
CPSIA Compliance Information: Batch BW18PK. For Further Information contact
Rosen Publishing, New York, New York at 1-800-237-9932.

CONTENTS

Words that appear like **this** can be found in the glossary on page 31.

Body Basics

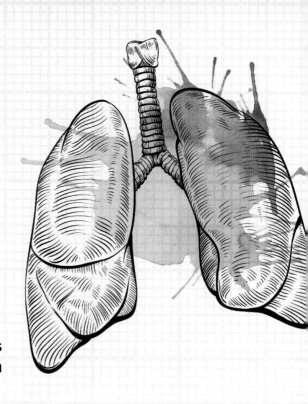

The body uses lots of systems. These systems are made up of different organs, and they help the body do the jobs that keep it healthy. All of the systems in the body have very important jobs to do, but some systems are more important than others. The four most important systems are:

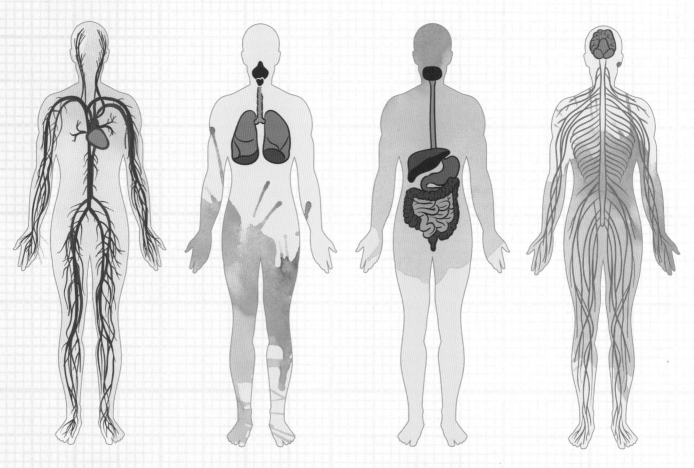

The circulatory system, which transports oxygen and nutrients around the body.

The respiratory system, which brings oxygen into the body.

The digestive system, which breaks down food and absorbs nutrients from it.

The nervous system, which sends information between the body and the brain.

There are also many important liquids in the body. The five main liquids in the body are blood, stomach acid, bile, mucus, and neurotransmitters.

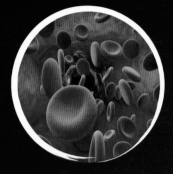

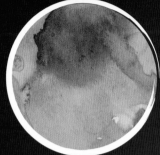

Blood helps the circulatory system to carry oxygen and nutrients.

Mucus stops the respiratory system from drying out and protects it from bacteria.

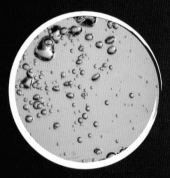

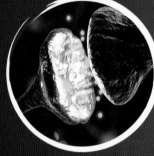

Stomach acid and bile help the digestive system to break down food.

Neurotransmitters help the nervous system to sort information in the brain.

THERE ARE 11 SYSTEMS IN THE BODY IN TOTAL.

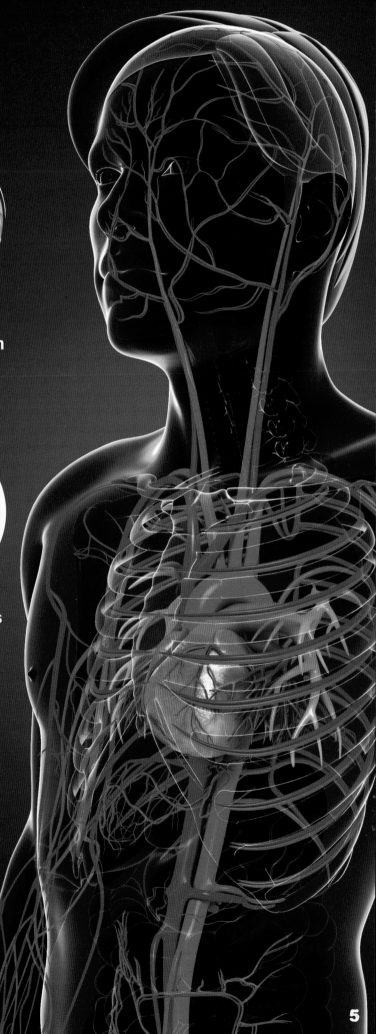

5

Beastly Blood

Every single one of us is filled with a beastly liquid called blood. It is probably the most important liquid in the entire body. It is made up of red blood cells, white blood cells, and platelets, which all help to keep your body healthy and protected.

Red Blood Cells

Red blood cells deliver oxygen and nutrients to every part of the body. They also pick up and carry away carbon dioxide, which is made by the body as it uses up energy.

Platelets

When you cut yourself, platelets come to the rescue. They block up holes in your skin to make sure that nasty invaders, such as germs and bacteria, don't get in and that your blood doesn't all gush out! They do this by attaching themselves to red blood cells and rolling up into a ball. This ball is then used to clog up the hole.

RED BLOOD CELLS

PLATELET

No matter how fast the platelets work, some bacterial invaders will always find their way into the body. But don't worry! They are dealt with by the body's own defense team — the white blood cells. These guys defend the body from invaders by hunting them down and eating them.

CLOTTING BLOOD

7

Popping Pus

Pus is one of the grossest things in the body. The thick, yellow liquid is made when white blood cells fight off bacterial invaders. During the battle, the bacteria release a deadly **toxin** to try to kill the white blood cells. If the invading bacteria are strong enough, they can cause an **infection**. Infections can eat away at your skin and leave a deep hole. This hole becomes filled with the bodies of white blood cells that died trying to protect the body. These white blood cells eventually become the ugliest and most hated liquid of them all — pus.

Stages of Pimple Growth

Acne is the most common condition that leads to pus. Acne occurs when bacteria enters a **hair follicle** and fights against the body's white blood cells. This results in small, pus-filled bumps known as pimples.

One of the most horrifying pus-filled wounds is an abscess. An abscess is an infection that causes pus to build up deep under the skin. Abscesses can grow to be over 1 inch (2 cm) in size. This causes the skin to become red and swollen. Thankfully, abscesses are much less common than acne and can be treated with **antibiotics**.

ABSCESS

IT'S VERY TEMPTING, BUT DON'T POP YOUR PIMPLES! IT WILL ONLY LET MORE NASTY BACTERIA INTO YOUR SKIN.

Messy Mucus

After pus, the next most disgusting and dreadful liquid in the body has to be mucus. It gets everywhere. Mucus is in your mouth, your throat, your lungs, and even your stomach. We sometimes call the mucus we get in our noses snot.

Mucus is mostly made out of water, but it also contains a pinch of salt, a sprinkling of dust, and most importantly, a couple of big squirts of mucins. Mucins are the things that make mucus gooey. They help mucus to complete its three jobs — making your insides slimy, catching dust, and killing bacteria.

MUCUS IS MADE UP OF:

WATER

DUST

MUCINS

SALT

WHITE BLOOD CELLS

Most of the time, your mucus is clear. However, when you're sick and your body is under attack from bacterial invaders, your mucus can become a horrible, green, gooey nightmare. Some people think the color of mucus changes because dead bacteria are floating about in it, but that's not true. Mucus turns green when it is filled with white blood cells.

OUR BODIES PRODUCE ABOUT 50 OUNCES (1.5 L) OF MUCUS EACH DAY, MOST OF WHICH GETS SWALLOWED!

Snot Simulation

Mucus is great at catching dust. Your throat is covered in a layer of the gooey stuff to stop anything from getting into your lungs. You can copy this effect with a fun and tasty experiment that involves making your own fake snot! Before you can create your own lick-able snot, you will need the following items:

20 grams of Plain Gelatin

Pinch of Salt

2 ounces (60 ml) of Corn Syrup

Green Food Coloring

Caster Sugar and Sprinkles

Wax Paper

Tape

Ice Cream (Optional)

Step 1)

Place the gelatin and salt into a heat-proof bowl and add in a few drops of the green food coloring. Pour 4 ounces (110 ml) of hot water into the heat-proof bowl. Gently stir the mixture with a fork. Add the corn syrup and stir the mixture again. Now, let it cool until it looks like snot. If it comes out too runny, add a little more gelatin.

Step 2)

Cut out a long strip of wax paper that is wide enough to roll into a tube. Spread the snot mixture onto the paper. Roll it into a tube and tape it closed.

Step 3)

Mix up two teaspoons of caster sugar and sprinkles. This will be your dust. Lay the tube down and blow half the dust down the tube. Turn the tube around and do it again.

Step 4)

Open the tube up and see how well your snot did. The sprinkles should have stuck to the fake snot, just as dust sticks to your mucus. Now, why not slap that dust-filled fake snot over some tasty ice cream? It wouldn't be snot if it didn't end up in your belly! Just don't wipe it on your sleeve.

Tangy Taste

To make sure that we don't eat anything nasty, our tongues have been armed with around 10,000 taste buds. These taste buds are tiny taste receptors that help you to detect and recognize different flavors. Taste receptors can sense five different flavors: sour, salty, bitter, sweet, and umami (which means savory flavors).

SOUR　　　**SALTY**　　　**BITTER**　　　**SWEET**　　　**UMAMI**

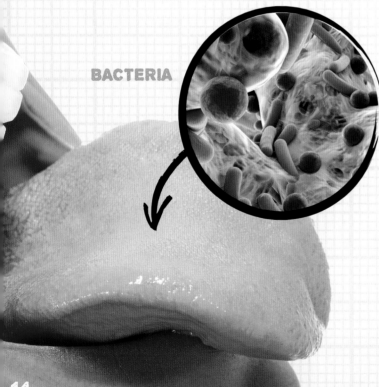

BACTERIA

Despite tasting all the delicious things that go into your mouth, the tongue actually has a brutal and difficult life. It is constantly exposed to the outside world, which means it's always being attacked by bacterial invaders. To protect itself from these invaders, the tongue covers itself with a slimy mucus called saliva. Saliva is filled with a deadly mix of bacteria-destroying chemicals. It also contains enzymes, which help to break down the food you eat.

Oral Thrush

Without saliva, your breath would smell worse than rotting meat. This is because saliva stops the tongue from drying out and becoming covered in bacteria. If your mouth did dry out, you could get oral thrush. This is when a foul-smelling, white fungus grows on the tongue. An easy way to avoid this oral horror is by eating less sugar.

Taste Test

Some people taste things differently from the rest of us. People who detect flavors more easily are called supertasters. They can do this because their tongue is covered with more taste receptors than most other people's. People who struggle to taste flavors are called non-tasters and they have fewer taste buds than the rest of us. What kind of taster are you? Find out with this easy experiment! You will need the following items:

COTTON SWAB

BLUE FOOD COLORING

HOLE PUNCHER

WAX PAPER

Step 1)

Use the hole puncher to make a hole in the wax paper. Now, dip the cotton bud into the blue food coloring. Use the cotton bud to cover a spot on your tongue about the size of your thumb.

Step 2)

The blue food coloring will slide off your taste buds and cause them to show up as pink dots. Place the wax paper with the hole in it over your tongue and use a mirror to count the pink dots inside the hole. Then check the number against the table below to find out what type of taster you are.

NUMBER OF PINK DOTS	TYPE OF TASTER	HOW COMMON IT IS
Fewer than 15	Non-taster	One in four people
Between 15 – 35	Average taster	Two in four people
More than 35	Supertaster	One in four people

Stomach Slush

The most disgusting liquids in the body have to be in the digestive system. Everything you swallow goes into your stomach. The stomach is the main organ in the digestive system. This is where food gets broken down by the stomach acid. The stomach also churns the food around. It squeezes and swirls the food like a washing machine, making sure that every bit of food is drenched in stomach acid.

Stomach acid is made of two substances — hydrochloric acid and enzymes. Hydrochloric acid breaks down big chunks of food into a smooth paste. The enzymes then break the food into **microscopic** parts. Once the food in the stomach has been dissolved into a runny slush, it is ready to be moved to the intestines.

Windy Waste

As soon as the slush from your stomach enters your small intestine, your body gets to work absorbing all the nutrients from it. To do this, the liver oozes out a dark, greenish-brown liquid called bile. Bile helps to break up the slush and makes it easier for the body to absorb all the good bits out of the food.

However, your digestive system wouldn't be able to do its job without its best friends — your gut flora. Your gut flora is a gang of bacteria that live in your gut. However, unlike a lot of bacteria, the ones in your gut flora are friendly and help your body to break down food. They also make the slush in your intestines smell really, really bad. When the bacteria break down the food in your gut, they release a smelly gas. This gas builds up and eventually forces its way out of your body. You might know this as "passing wind."

GUT FLORA

INTESTINE LINING

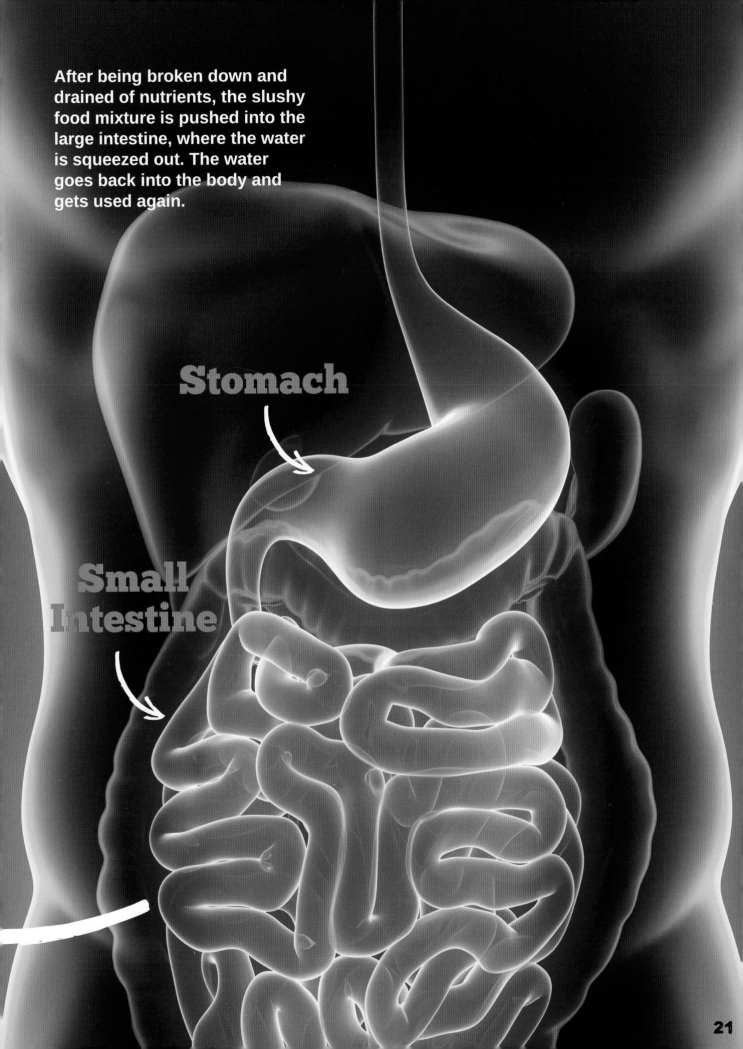

After being broken down and drained of nutrients, the slushy food mixture is pushed into the large intestine, where the water is squeezed out. The water goes back into the body and gets used again.

Stomach

Small Intestine

Buzzing Brain

The idea of a body without a brain is unthinkable. (Unthinkable... Get it? Never mind.) The brain is like a big computer that tells the body what to do. It is home to all the thoughts and feelings that make you who you are. It's the brain's job to understand all the information that it gets from the body and to react to this information in the best way possible.

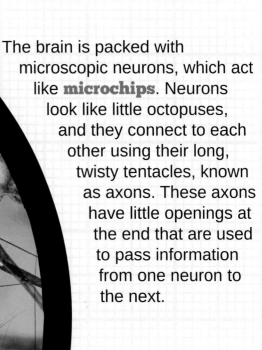

The brain is packed with microscopic neurons, which act like **microchips**. Neurons look like little octopuses, and they connect to each other using their long, twisty tentacles, known as axons. These axons have little openings at the end that are used to pass information from one neuron to the next.

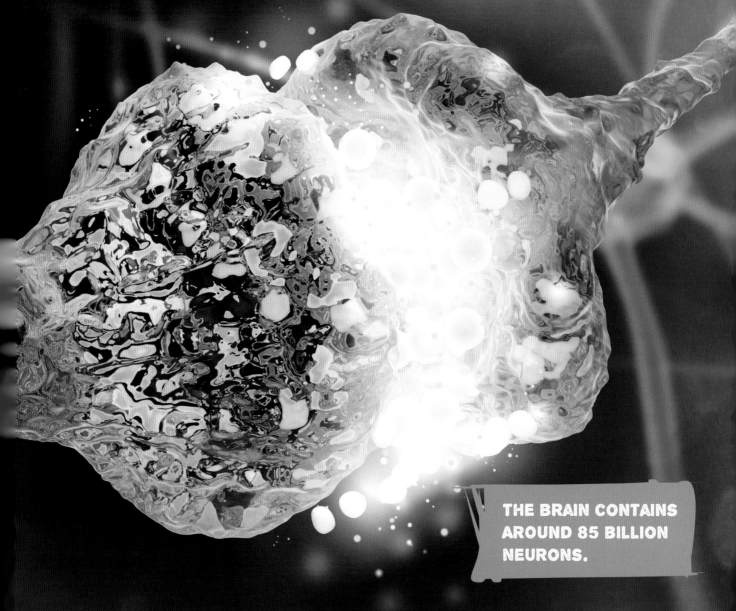

Neurons pass information around the brain using special brain-chemicals known as neurotransmitters. Small electrical charges run through the neurons, and this gives them the energy to pass information to each other. This means that everything you do, from clapping your hands to stamping your feet, is controlled by neurons, neurotransmitters, and small electrical charges. Weird, right?

Don't worry if all this talk about chemicals in the brain is a bit confusing. Not even the best scientists in the world understand everything about the brain — it's just too complicated!

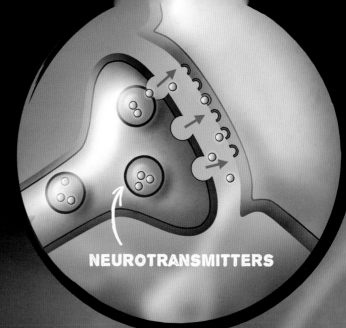

NEUROTRANSMITTERS

THE BRAIN CONTAINS AROUND 85 BILLION NEURONS.

Brain Blunders

Thinking is hard work, so our brains will often make the job easier by making **assumptions**. Most of the time, these assumptions help us to do things faster. However, they can sometimes cause us to see things in a strange way. Have a look at the optical illusions on the next page and see if you can tell what your brain is doing wrong.

1. When looking at the first picture, your brain doesn't realize that the image is flat. The lines drawn across the picture make your brain see a long corridor. Because of this, your brain thinks that the man on the right is standing behind the other two men.

Your brain also knows that people farther away should look smaller, but the man on the right doesn't look smaller. This makes the brain assume that the man on the right must actually be a lot bigger than the other men! In reality, they are all the same size.

2. Look at the dotted squares in the second picture. The square under the shadow looks lighter than the square above it. This is because your brain can see the pattern of the floor and assumes that the center square must be light in color, like the other squares. However, cover up all the other squares and you will see that they are, in fact, exactly the same color.

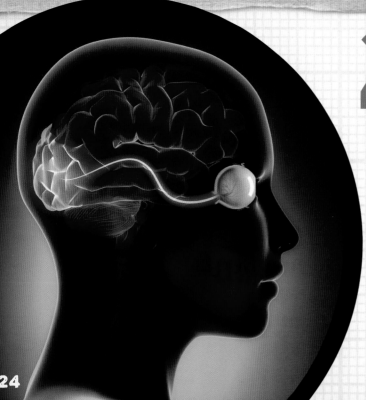

1.

2.

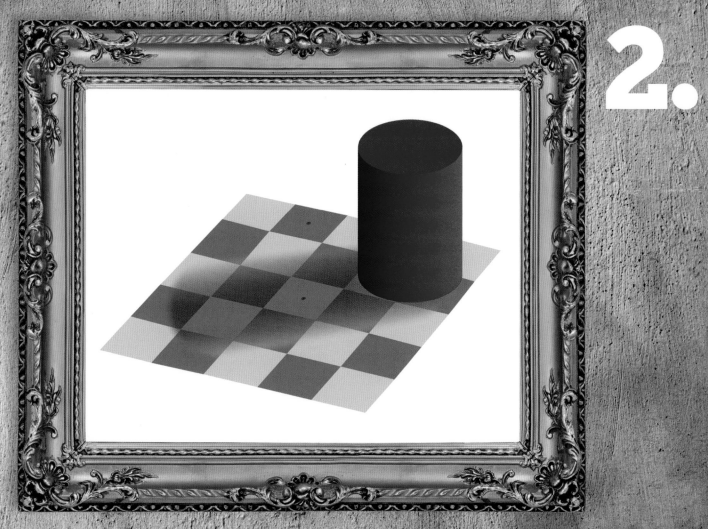

Despicable Doctors

Andreas Vesalius

Date of Birth: Dec 31, 1514

Date of Death: Oct 15, 1564

Place of Birth: Belgium

Hobbies: Brushing his beard and cutting up human bodies.

When Andreas Vesalius was alive, medical books used animals to show how the human body worked. This was because cutting open human bodies after they had died was seen as a ghastly and evil thing to do. Also, people assumed that animals' bodies all worked in exactly the same way. Spoiler alert — they don't.

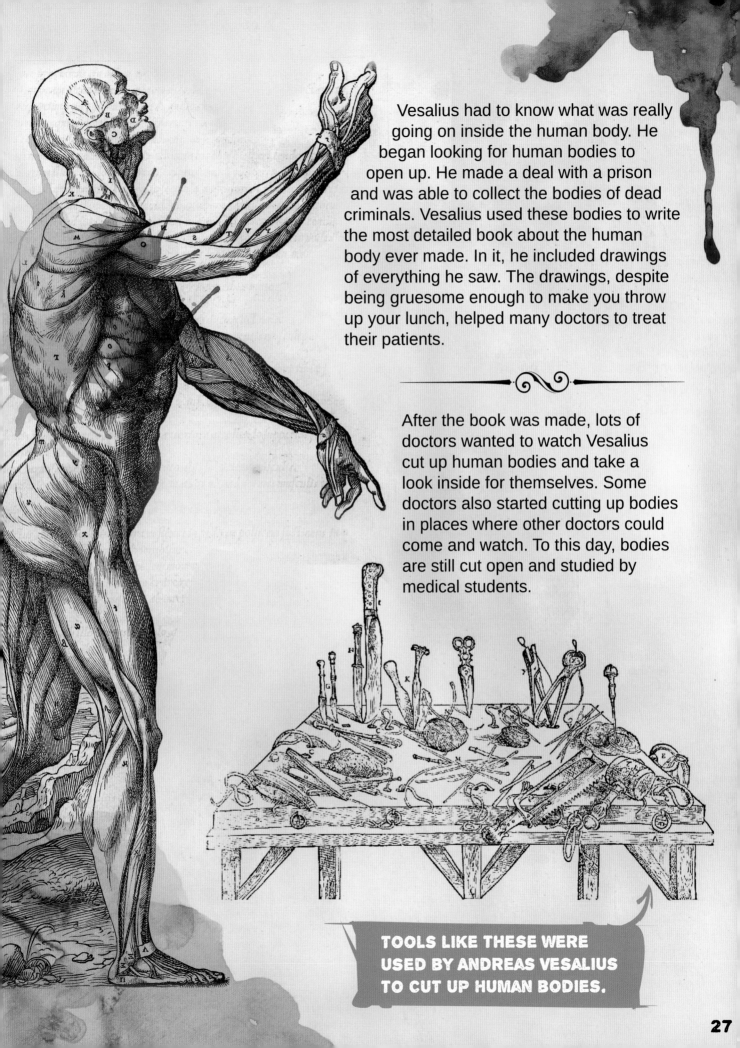

Vesalius had to know what was really going on inside the human body. He began looking for human bodies to open up. He made a deal with a prison and was able to collect the bodies of dead criminals. Vesalius used these bodies to write the most detailed book about the human body ever made. In it, he included drawings of everything he saw. The drawings, despite being gruesome enough to make you throw up your lunch, helped many doctors to treat their patients.

After the book was made, lots of doctors wanted to watch Vesalius cut up human bodies and take a look inside for themselves. Some doctors also started cutting up bodies in places where other doctors could come and watch. To this day, bodies are still cut open and studied by medical students.

TOOLS LIKE THESE WERE USED BY ANDREAS VESALIUS TO CUT UP HUMAN BODIES.

Edward Jenner

Date of Birth: May 17, 1749

Date of Death: Jan 26, 1823

Place of Birth: England

Hobbies: Bird watching and **injecting** children with diseases.

Hundreds of years ago, a disease called smallpox swept through Europe. It caused people's bodies to become covered in pus-filled bumps before eventually killing them. But Edward Jenner noticed something very peculiar — **milkmaids** almost never got smallpox. He believed that this was because many of them had caught a similar disease found in cows, called cowpox. This disease was not as dangerous to humans.

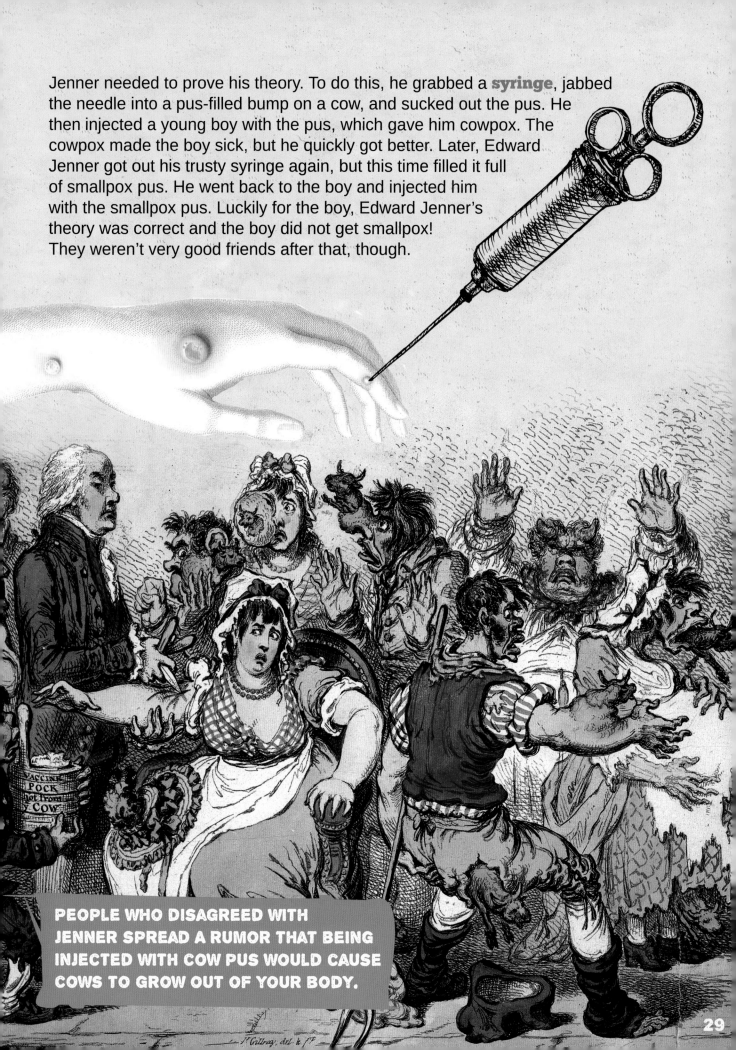

Jenner needed to prove his theory. To do this, he grabbed a **syringe**, jabbed the needle into a pus-filled bump on a cow, and sucked out the pus. He then injected a young boy with the pus, which gave him cowpox. The cowpox made the boy sick, but he quickly got better. Later, Edward Jenner got out his trusty syringe again, but this time filled it full of smallpox pus. He went back to the boy and injected him with the smallpox pus. Luckily for the boy, Edward Jenner's theory was correct and the boy did not get smallpox! They weren't very good friends after that, though.

PEOPLE WHO DISAGREED WITH JENNER SPREAD A RUMOR THAT BEING INJECTED WITH COW PUS WOULD CAUSE COWS TO GROW OUT OF YOUR BODY.

QUICK QUIZ

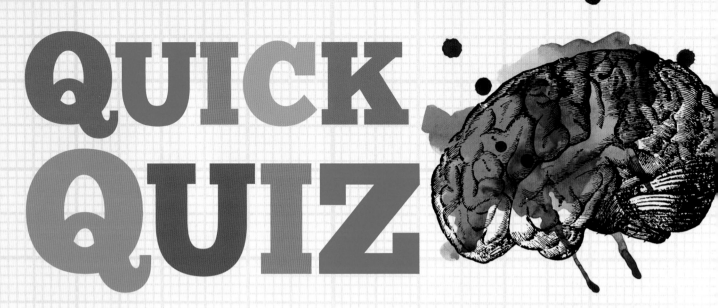

HAVE YOU TAKEN IT ALL IN? TAKE THIS QUICK QUIZ TO TEST YOUR KNOWLEDGE. THE ANSWERS ARE UPSIDE DOWN AT THE BOTTOM OF THE PAGE.

1. What part of blood helps to block up holes in the skin?

2. What is pus made of?

3. What type of mucus covers your tongue?

4. What is it on your tongue that detects flavors?

5. What are the three main jobs of mucus?

6. What part of the body absorbs the nutrients out of food?

7. What are the chemicals in the brain called?

8. What did Andreas Vesalius do to dead human bodies?

9. Which disease did Edward Jenner stop with cow pus?

10. What type of taster are you?

1) Platelets 2) Dead white blood cells 3) Saliva 4) Taste buds 5) Keeping things slimy (wet), catching dust, and killing bacteria 6) The intestines 7) Neurotransmitters 8) Cut them open 9) Smallpox 10) Did you forget? Find out by doing the experiment on page 16.

GLOSSARY

acid	a liquid that can break down objects into small pieces
antibiotics	a medicine that stops germs and other small living things from growing in the body
assumptions	beliefs that are accepted as true without any proof
bacteria	microscopic living things
enzymes	chemicals made by living things that break down substances
hair follicle	the area beneath the skin that surrounds the root of a hair
infection	an invasion of bacteria that are not normally in the body
injecting	putting into the body using a syringe
microchips	small parts of computers that sort through information
microscopic	so small it can only be seen with a microscope
milkmaids	women who milk cows
nutrients	natural substances that people need in order to grow and stay healthy
oral	to do with or relating to the mouth
organs	(self-contained) parts of a living thing that have specific, important functions
oxygen	a natural gas that all living things need in order to survive
syringe	a device with a long needle at the end, used for injecting liquids into the body
toxin	a poison made by a living thing

INDEX